LET'S THINK ABOUT

the Internet and Social Media

Alex Woolf

Raintree is an imprint of Capstone Global Library Limited, a company incorporated in England and Wales having its registered office at 7 Pilgrim Street, London, EC4V 6LB – Registered company number: 6695582

www.raintreepublishers.co.uk
myorders@raintreepublishers.co.uk

Edited by John Paul Wilkins, Clare Lewis, and Kathryn Clay
Designed by Tim Bond and Peggie Carley
Picture research by Liz Alexander and Tracy Cummins
Production by Victoria Fitzgerald
Originated by Capstone Global Library Ltd
Printed and bound in China by CTPS

ISBN 978 1 406 28265 8
18 17 16 15 14
10 9 8 7 6 5 4 3 2 1

British Library Cataloguing in Publication Data
A full catalogue record for this book is available from the British Library.

Acknowledgements
We would like to thank the following for permission to reproduce photographs:
Alamy: © Chris Rout, 22, © digitallife, 19, © dpa picture alliance archive, 26, © epa european pressphoto agency b.v., 27, 30, © Geoffrey Robinson, 33, © imagebroker, 31, © Jochen Tack, 35, © Peter Phipp/Travelshots.com, 12, © Stuwdamdorp, 15 bottom; Dreamstime: Katatonia82, 20, R. Eko Bintoro, 11; Getty Images: Adrian Pope, 43, AFP PHOTO/ BELGA PHOTO BENOIT DOPPAGNE, 42, AFP PHOTO/GABRIEL BOUYS 29, AFP PHOTO/ JUNG YEON-JE, 8, AFP PHOTO/KHALED DESOUKI, 25, Dimitri Otis, front cover, James Keyser//Time Life Pictures, 7, Spencer Platt, 38; Google: 39; iStock: Empato, 15 top; Science Photo Library: CERN, 6; Shutterstock: Annette Shaff, 40, Goodluz, 5, 36, Lucky Business, 28, Monkey Business Images, 16; Wikipedia: (Wikipedia(R) and its Wikipedia puzzle globe(R) are official trademarks of the Wikimedia Foundation in the United States and other countries. These marks are being used under license by the Wikimedia Foundation. This book is not endorsed by or affiliated with the Wikimedia Foundation), 13

Every effort has been made to contact copyright holders of material reproduced in this book. Any omissions will be rectified in subsequent printings if notice is given to the publisher.

Contents

Some words are shown in bold, **like this**.
You can find out what they mean by looking in the glossary.

The internet and social media: what are the issues?

Sometimes it's difficult to appreciate a revolution when you're in the middle of it. But have no doubt, we *are* in a revolution right now – the internet revolution. And it's at least as important as the printing revolution of 500 years ago.

Before the internet

The internet is changing almost every part of our lives, including the way we work, study, shop, socialize and have fun. The easiest way to understand this is to look at how we lived before the internet became popular. Before the early 1990s, if you wanted to research something for school, your only option was to go to a library and find a book about it. If you wanted to buy something, you had to go to a shop. If you wanted to communicate with friends, you could phone them, write them a letter or visit them.

A good thing?

Of course, we can still do all these things. But the internet has expanded our options. At the same time, the internet has made everything much more convenient. And that makes it a good thing ... or does it? This book will look at the ways in which the internet and social media have changed our lives for the better, as well as the problems and dangers of the online world.

DID YOU KNOW?

In 1995, 16 million people used the internet (0.4 percent of the world's population). In 2013 internet users numbered 2.7 billion (38.8 percent of the world's population).

What are the internet and social media?

What is the internet?

The internet is a worldwide network of computers that are all linked together. Computers communicate by sending each other small packets of digital data. The data travels across the internet according to a set of rules called TCP/IP. These packets travel at incredible speeds, allowing us to connect with people around the world in seconds.

How it all began

The internet began in 1969 when the US Defense Department built the world's first computer network, called ARPANET. At first there were just four computers on ARPANET. The TCP/IP rules for connecting computers were developed in the mid 1970s. By 1986 there were 5,000 computers on the network.

This NeXT computer ran the first World Wide Web server in 1990.

In the early 1990s, police used the internet to track down criminals.

The World Wide Web

Computer scientist Tim Berners-Lee invented a system in 1990 that would change the internet into a tool that anyone could use. He did this by joining **hypertext** with the internet to create a network of linked pages. Navigating the internet suddenly became much easier. Berners-Lee called it the World Wide Web (WWW). He made the technology freely available so anyone could use it.

DID YOU KNOW?

The first message ever sent on ARPANET was "lo." Student programmer Charley Kline sent the message at 10.30 p.m. on 29 October 1969. He had meant to say "login," but the system crashed before it could send it to the rest of the word.

Browsers and search engines

In the early 1990s the internet and WWW were still used mainly by universities and the military. In 1993 the arrival of easy-to-use **browsers** using point-and-click **icons** meant ordinary people could "surf the Net". As the internet grew in popularity, the number of web pages began to multiply.

As the WWW expanded, so did the need for **search engines** to help users find what they needed. The first search engine that allowed users to search for any word on a web page was WebCrawler. Others quickly followed, including Yahoo and Netscape. Since 2000 Google has been the world's most popular search engine.

Vinton Cerf is considered a founding father of the internet. Since 2005 he has served as Google's vice president.

WHAT DO YOU THINK?

Do you think the rise of the internet has been a good thing for society? Try to imagine living in the world before the World Wide Web. In what ways would your life be better? How might it be worse?

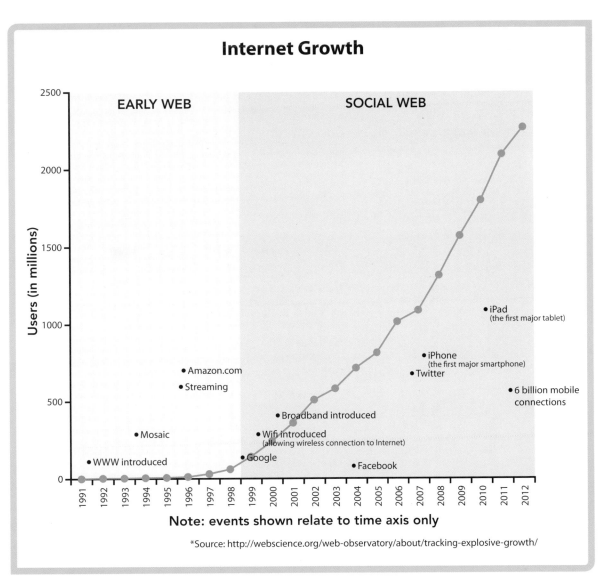

Internet Growth

EARLY WEB

SOCIAL WEB

Users (in millions)

- iPad (the first major tablet)
- iPhone (the first major smartphone)
- Twitter
- 6 billion mobile connections
- Amazon.com
- Streaming
- Broadband introduced
- Mosaic
- Wifi introduced (allowing wireless connection to Internet)
- WWW introduced
- Google
- Facebook

Note: events shown relate to time axis only

*Source: http://webscience.org/web-observatory/about/tracking-explosive-growth/

Broadband

The internet was quite slow during the early years. Even today's slowest computers are 20 times faster. People had to connect using a phone line, and it took hours to **download** anything but text. Downloading a movie would have taken up to five days!

The arrival of **broadband** in the early 2000s gave another big boost to the internet. With dramatically improved connection speeds, it opened up a new world of online TV shows, films and games. Around the same time, **smartphones** and **tablets** began appearing that could connect to the internet wirelessly. In 2015 and beyond, it's likely that more people will be using the internet on mobile devices than on desktop computers.

History

In its early years, the WWW was a place of basic websites that people would view in the same way they watched TV. This began to change in the late 1990s when users began creating their own content in the form of **blogs** and **social networks**. By the early 2000s, the WWW had become a place where people could share, discuss, and co-create new content.

What is social media?

Social media is a term used to describe all the ways in which we socialize with each other online. This table shows the different types of social media.

internet forums:	online discussion sites where people have conversations in the form of posted messages
chat rooms:	websites where people have conversations in real-time using instant messaging
blogs:	websites where articles are posted online by an individual or group
wikis:	websites that allow people to add, change or delete content in collaboration with others, such as Wikipedia
social networks:	websites that allow people to make friends, communicate, and share ideas, pictures, activities, events, and interests, such as Facebook
microblogs:	similar to blogs except the entries are restricted to a certain number of characters to keep them short, such as Twitter

CYBER SENSE

When participating in an internet forum, chat room or other form of social media, here are some basic rules to remember.

- Avoid personal abuse. It's OK to disagree with people, but don't threaten them or call them names.

- Remember that your posts are public and can be read by anyone.

- Stay on topic. Don't post about football in a fashion forum.

How the internet helps us with our work

People used to go to libraries to find information. Now if we want to find out something, we "google" it. Without question the internet has changed the way we study and work. But are there any negatives to these changes?

Up to date

The internet is a fantastic source of information on every subject you can think of. Unlike printed books and magazines, the internet can include video alongside text and illustrations. It can also be updated constantly, giving us the latest developments in whatever interests us.

Interactive

Because the internet is interactive, we can focus on information that's most important to us. For example, we can enter our post codes to find out the weather in our neighbourhoods. With tools such as search engines and **hyperlinks**, we can access the information we need quickly and easily.

Global

The internet is a global super-library available to everyone with access to broadband, no matter where they live. It's a place where people in different parts of the world can work together on projects for school, work or general interest. In all these ways, the internet has advantages over books.

DID YOU KNOW?

With 30 million articles in 286 languages and an estimated 365 million readers worldwide, Wikipedia is the world's largest general knowledge resource. The site was launched in 2001 and is written by volunteers around the world. Anyone with access to the site can edit the articles.

Accuracy

One strength of the internet is its openness. Anyone can **upload** content. But this can be a problem when you're using the internet for research. For most research projects, we can generally trust books. Books, after all, are usually written by professional authors and have editors and consultants checking the facts. But how can we trust the internet if anyone can upload content? The information may be inaccurate, **biased** or out of date.

We can't ignore information on the internet just because some of it might be incorrect. But how can we be sure the information we find is accurate?

Assessing online information

Think about the purpose of the website where you found the information. Does it belong to a business that's trying to sell you something? Or is it a political site that's trying to persuade you to think in a particular way? If so, the information it contains may be biased.

Is the website poorly written and designed? That's often a clue that the information may be untrustworthy. Does it list its sources? Reliable websites should include a list of books, articles and other sources where they got their information. Finally, if the site's author is not identified or the site has not been recently updated, you may want to avoid it.

WHAT DO YOU THINK?

Do you think sites that allow anyone to change them might sometimes be useful sources of information? What about **user-generated websites**? How do you make sure the information you use from the internet is accurate?

Politicians use the internet to share campaign information.

Reliable websites

Where should you go to find trustworthy information? It's best to rely on sites belonging to respected public institutions such as museums, public service broadcasters (such as the BBC) and universities. Google Books and Google Scholar allow you to search the content of millions of books and magazines and are also very reliable. User-generated sites, such as Wikipedia, may be useful as part of your research. But remember that anyone can edit content, so it's always best to double-check any facts gathered there.

Distraction danger

There are other drawbacks to internet-based research. It may be easy to find information online, but it isn't necessarily a good place for reading more about a subject. Reading from a screen can be hard on the eyes after a while. It's also easy to link to other pages and become distracted by the things you find there. As a result, the internet could be weakening our powers of concentration. People who do all their research online may end up with a widespread knowledge about many things, but perhaps not a very in-depth one.

CYBER SAFETY

Using a computer for long periods without a break can cause health problems. Here are some tips to stay healthy.

- Avoid straining your eyes by looking away from the screen from time to time. Close your eyes to reset moisture levels.

- Avoid back pain by keeping your back straight, feet flat on the floor, and thighs and forearms parallel to the floor.

- Avoid carpal tunnel syndrome (a disorder caused by repeated movement of hands and fingers) by minimizing use of the mouse. Find keyboard shortcuts, and regularly stretch and massage your hands.

How social media helps us connect with people

Today we use social media to hang out with our friends, meet new friends or reconnect with old ones. As a result, a big part of our social lives is spent in front of a screen.

Our online identity

Social media sites encourage users to create an online identity. Users share personal details and blog about their lives. They upload pictures and videos and form groups with others. Increasingly, people can share their profiles, photos, videos and blogs between different social media sites. For example, people use Facebook, Twitter and Instagram to form one overall online identity.

DID YOU KNOW?

Social networking site Facebook was founded in 2004 by Harvard University student Mark Zuckerburg. Ten years later, more than 1.11 billion users had signed up for accounts.

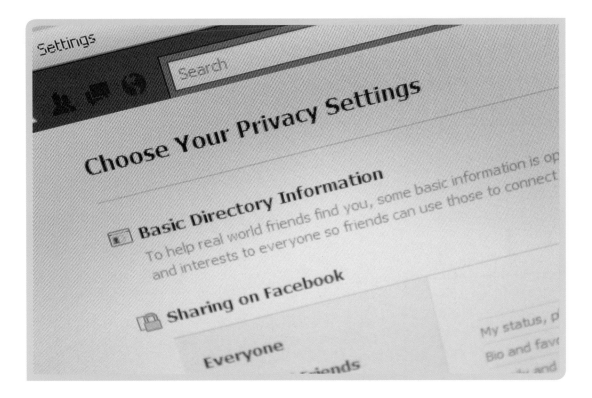

Privacy issues

There are dangers to sharing personal information with a wide group of people. It can reveal things that you'd rather your teachers or future employers didn't know. For example, someone who applied for a job at a business in Chicago, U.S.A. was turned down because of references to illegal activity found on his Facebook page.

Posting information about yourself can also put your personal safety at risk. The information could end up in the hands of strangers who might want to hurt you or steal from you. One teenager from New York posted on various social media sites that her family was going on holiday. Burglars saw her posts, worked out when her home would be empty, and broke in.

Too much information

Young people are more willing than ever to post personal information on social media sites. Information might include their birth date, home town and school. According to one survey, about 20 percent even share their phone numbers. Posting this kind of information makes it easy to be tracked by strangers with bad intentions.

Some sites allow people to **stream** photos live while at an event. Sites such as Foursquare allow users to "check in" to places using the GPS in their phones. This may be useful for you and your friends, but it also means that anyone knows where you are and when.

Real-time web

Chat rooms, instant messaging, and live streaming allow people to send and receive texts and images in real time. These sites can bring users into contact with people they don't know and can't physically see. It allows adults to pose as children in chat rooms. This danger has become such a big problem that police have posed as teenagers online in order to catch such adults.

CYBER SAFETY

Here are some tips to stay safe when using social media.

- Keep your password private.
- Only give your phone number, email and home address to trusted friends.
- Use **privacy settings** to restrict the number of people who see your personal information.
- Be careful about meeting anyone you've only met online. If you absolutely trust the person, make sure you meet in a public place during the day. Always bring an adult with you.

Online behaviour

From the privacy of your bedroom, it's easy to forget that the internet is a public space. Information uploaded there is permanent. Once the information is out there, it's often impossible to take back. For that reason, people need to take personal responsibility for the content they upload. They should avoid posting anything that will hurt, anger, or scare people. In extreme cases, it may become a matter for the police. In February 2013 teenager Justin Carter jokingly threatened to carry out a school shooting. He was arrested and sent to prison.

Cyberbullying

Some people use social media sites as a means of bullying people. **Cyberbullies** send mean or threatening messages. They create hostile websites, post incorrect information to blogs or upload embarrassing photos of their victims.

Psychological effects

Does the use of social media damage us? Some people argue that social networking can become addictive. People feel the need to stay connected all the time in case they miss out on something important. Too much time spent online can lead to self-obsession, anxiety, depression and problems with concentration. People also tend to put only the best bits of their lives online. Sometimes it can seem that other people's lives are a lot better than our own. On the other hand, social media can make it easier for shy people to build social relationships.

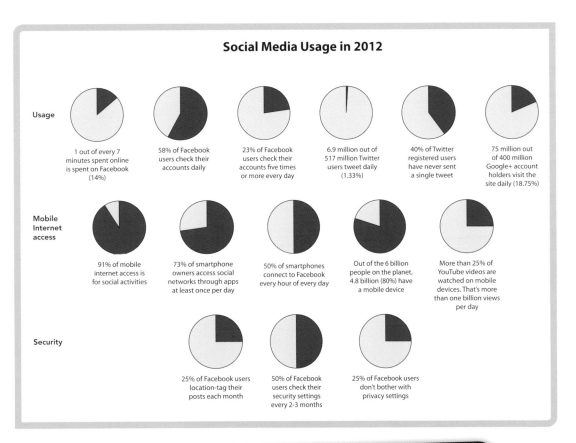

Social Media Usage in 2012

Usage
- 1 out of every 7 minutes spent online is spent on Facebook (14%)
- 58% of Facebook users check their accounts daily
- 23% of Facebook users check their accounts five times or more every day
- 6.9 million out of 517 million Twitter users tweet daily (1.33%)
- 40% of Twitter registered users have never sent a single tweet
- 75 million out of 400 million Google+ account holders visit the site daily (18.75%)

Mobile Internet access
- 91% of mobile internet access is for social activities
- 73% of smartphone owners access social networks through apps at least once per day
- 50% of smartphones connect to Facebook every hour of every day
- Out of the 6 billion people on the planet, 4.8 billion (80%) have a mobile device
- More than 25% of YouTube videos are watched on mobile devices. That's more than one billion views per day

Security
- 25% of Facebook users location-tag their posts each month
- 50% of Facebook users check their security settings every 2-3 months
- 25% of Facebook users don't bother with privacy settings

WHAT DO YOU THINK?

How much time do you spend each week on social media sites? How do you feel after using these sites? Is your time online always fun?

A political tool

People are increasingly using social media to try to get support for particular causes, such as political campaigns and protests. Blogs and social networking sites can be used to encourage large groups of like-minded people to take part. One example is the Occupy movement. Activists protesting against social and economic inequality use social media such as Internet Relay Chat (IRC), Facebook, Twitter and Meetup to organize events.

Clicktivism

Social media also encourages a less active form of protest known as clicktivism. Clicktivists might do no more than "like" or share a Facebook page or forward a pre-written message as a way of showing their support. By asking so little of people, protest movements can show impressive numbers of supporters. However, few people are prepared to take real action.

DID YOU KNOW?

Social media can often be a force for good. In January 2013 professional football player Angel Rangel was buying a sandwich when the shop owner mentioned he would have to throw away a lot of leftover food. Rangel tweeted a message to his 24,000 followers saying, "Anyone knows the location of homeless people in Swansea? I got food going spare!" Many people responded, and Rangel handed over the food to a local homeless shelter.

In 2011 Facebook became an important way for Egyptian protesters to organize and share information.

Twitter revolution

In some countries the government controls the TV, radio and newspapers but has less control over social media. People living in such countries can use social media as a form of protest. They can share videos of government violence, organize street demonstrations, send worldwide messages, and stir up international anger. Social media was used a great deal in the Egyptian Revolution of 2011, when a popular uprising led to the overthrow of the government. One activist tweeted, "We use Facebook to schedule the protests, Twitter to coordinate, and YouTube to tell the world."

Using the internet and social media for entertainment

The internet has changed the way we enjoy music and entertainment. Today fewer CDs and DVDs are purchased. People prefer to download or stream videos and music directly on their computers or mobile devices.

Opportunities for new artists

Before the internet young musicians would have to be signed by a record label in order to get their music heard. Music industry executives had the power to make or break new bands.

The internet has enabled young musicians to be seen and heard – including surprising or unusual personalities who might not have had much chance in the past. One example is Kim Yeo-Hee, better known as Apple Girl. Yeo-Hee gained fame through her uploaded videos in 2010. She uses Apple iPhones as instruments to create backup music for her singing.

In 2012 Psy's music video for the song "Gangnam Style" was the first YouTube video to reach 1 billion views.

A driving force behind this development has been YouTube, the user-generated video-sharing website. Music and entertainment videos uploaded on to YouTube can reach large audiences.

Those who shout loudest

The very openness of the internet means that anyone can find an audience. Often it's those with a talent for promoting themselves that get heard rather than those with a talent for music. The other problem is that the massive quantity of material available online can be overwhelming for people.

DID YOU KNOW?

In 2008 Canadian pop star Justin Bieber shot to worldwide fame, aged 14. Talent manager Scooter Braun found his videos on YouTube. By June 2013 Bieber's YouTube videos had been viewed 2.8 billion times. He had 46 million Facebook fans, more than 40 million followers on Twitter, and had sold more than 15 million albums.

Online piracy

One major problem faced by the entertainment industry as a result of social media is online piracy. This is the illegal selling or sharing of material, such as music, games or videos, without the permission of the owners of that material. The most common form of online piracy is **peer-to-peer file sharing**, which is when people copy computer files from one computer to another to avoid paying for them. This began in 1999 with the arrival of Napster, the first file-sharing website.

Some claim that peer-to-peer file sharing has cost the music industry billions of pounds in profits. Others say that those who download music illegally wouldn't necessarily have purchased the music legally anyway. They argue that illegal downloading actually encourages sales. Illegal downloading is now decreasing, perhaps due to the popularity of streaming services such as Spotify.

WHAT DO YOU THINK?

Do you think it's OK to file share or enjoy music and entertainment you haven't paid for?

1
TWEETS

8
ABON

Pope Francis @Pontifex

Pope Francis has more than 1.6 million Twitter followers.

Celebrities and social media

Celebrities are using social media sites such as YouTube, Twitter, Facebook and Spotify to create a direct link to their fans. Facebook, with its "like" and "share" options, allows songs, videos and news to spread **virally**. This type of sharing among friends increases exposure for celebrities and their material.

Celebrities share personal and professional information on social media as a way of promoting themselves. Daily tweets help keep them in the public eye. Lady Gaga tweets hints about upcoming albums and tours to keep her fans guessing. For misbehaving celebrities, social media has become the place where they apologize and explain themselves. For everyone else, it's an endless source of entertaining celebrity news.

Celebrity-fan relationships

From a fan's point of view, social media is an opportunity to feel much closer to their heroes. This is very different from pre-internet days when celebrities existed in their own remote world. Now their public images are carefully controlled by managers and public relations (PR) consultants.

Some people argue that the accessibility of today's stars removes some of their mystery. It also places celebrities at risk of receiving unwanted attention from obsessive fans and **stalkers**. Some sites even track the movements of famous people and send users a mobile alert when one is nearby. These sites seem to suggest that celebrities have absolutely no right to a private life.

In 2011 Joss Stone was the target of two obsessed fans. The men were arrested before they could harm her.

CYBER SAFETY

Here are some tips for staying safe when playing online games.

- Only play online games if your device is running up-to-date antivirus software.

- Only play authorized versions of games bought from trustworthy sites.

- Do not reveal any personal information to other players. Use a nickname for your username.

- If another player is behaving badly, block him or her.

A study by Spil Games reported that 1.2 billion people played online games in 2013.

Online gaming

In recent years more people began playing video games online. Online gaming allows players to play with other gamers around the world, often for free. Online games can be simple text-based environments or games with complex graphics and virtual worlds.

Many online games create **virtual communities** that turn gaming into a much more social experience. But like all communities, online gaming groups must cope with bad behaviour by other users. There are instances of cheating, cyberbullying, trolling (unpleasant posts), spamming (irrelevant or inappropriate messages) and rude language.

Buying and selling on the internet

The internet has become an enormous marketplace for people and businesses to buy and sell to each other. There are auction sites such as eBay, online advertising networks such as Gumtree, as well as large online shops such as Amazon. Online trading can be a positive experience for some. For others, it can lead to disappointment.

Selling online

The internet has made the process of selling much easier for ordinary people. Auction or advertising sites can reach far more possible buyers than newspaper advertisements and can raise a lot more money.

The main danger with online selling is that you are dealing with strangers. If you have something to sell, get your parents to help you. When placing an ad, never list your full name, address or phone number. If you have to meet a buyer to let them inspect the item or to complete the sale, do so in a public place, and always go there with a trusted adult.

Advantages of shopping online

Online shopping is fast and convenient. Bargain hunters appreciate the easy comparisons between online shops. Customers can read reviews of products before they buy them. Online shopping also frees customers from the effort of a trip to the shops or of having to shop during business hours. Online shops are usually open 24 hours a day.

Some Amazon warehouses are as large as 14 football fields.

DID YOU KNOW?

Amazon.com is the world's largest online shop, responsible for about one-third of all US online sales. Founder Jeff Bezos originally planned to call it Cadabra.

Disadvantages

Online shopping is not quite the same as shopping or browsing in an actual shop. Nor can it match the fun of real-world shopping with friends. The virtual assistants on shopping sites cannot yet match the human qualities of real-life shop assistants. The fact that you can't look at the actual product before buying it can be problematic when buying food or clothes. Products bought online must also be delivered, so there's a delay before receiving the items. There's usually a delivery cost, too.

Impact on main-street shops

Most big retail chains now sell their products online as well. As a result, the internet has driven many independent shops out of existence. Simply put, fewer people do their buying in a **brick-and-mortar** shop. People who do all their shopping online may not mean to harm these smaller shops. But this is the result of online competition.

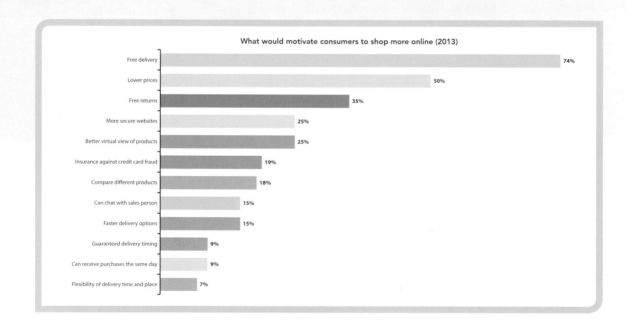

What would motivate consumers to shop more online (2013)

Free delivery	74%
Lower prices	50%
Free returns	35%
More secure websites	25%
Better virtual view of products	25%
Insurance against credit card fraud	19%
Compare different products	18%
Can chat with sales person	15%
Faster delivery options	15%
Guaranteed delivery timing	9%
Can receive purchases the same day	9%
Flexibility of delivery time and place	7%

Credit card fraud

One disadvantage of online shopping is the danger of **fraud**. When customers hand over their credit card details, they must trust the website and its employees not to steal this information. **Hackers** present another danger. They might break into the shop's website and steal credit card details.

WHAT DO YOU THINK?

Do you prefer online or traditional shopping? Why? Does it matter that online shopping affects the sales of smaller, local businesses?

Problems with purchase

With online shopping, customers have to trust the website to actually deliver the item. What if it doesn't arrive, it's not what was expected, or it's damaged? Each country has its own laws to protect customers. Usually, if the purchase was made with a credit card, then the seller must give the buyer his or her money back. If the seller refuses or can't be found, then the credit card company must issue a refund.

Taking care

Unfortunately, the world of online shopping provides many opportunities for **scammers**, frauds, and thieves. Some have professional-looking websites and pretend to be real online shops. This act is called phishing. Others try to steal identities or secretly access customers' **hard drives** to track their movements on the web.

We need to be watchful at all times when buying online. Be especially cautious of sellers who request up-front payments or offer incredible bargains. Remember the golden rule – if it sounds too good to be true, then it probably is.

CYBER SAFETY

Customers should protect themselves by only buying from trustworthy websites. If unsure about a particular website, they can easily check on them by completing an online search. If buying from an online auction site, check seller ratings and reviews to see how reliable or efficient they are.

When entering credit card details, the web page address should begin "https" rather than just "http". The "s" indicates that the information being sent is **encrypted**. After the purchase customers should check their credit card statements to make sure the price is as expected.

Always remember to ask adults for permission before using their credit cards.

Environmental costs of using the internet

Whether we're sending messages, surfing or watching videos, we're using electricity. With more than 1.7 billion people online at any one time, this is having an impact on the environment.

Expanding energy footprint

Much of the electricity we use comes from burning fossil fuels. When fossil fuels are burned, they emit a gas called carbon dioxide. These emissions add to pollution and are a major cause of human-created global warming. Our use of computers accounts for around two percent of global emissions of carbon dioxide.

Experts estimate that the energy footprint of the internet is growing by more than 10 percent each year and is now greater than the airline industry. But the environmental impact of the internet isn't only from the energy used by our computers. It also comes from the sending and storing of data.

In some places in Africa the environment has been impacted by the mining of tantalum, a mineral used in mobile phones and tablets.

Blue LED lights on servers are energy efficient and bright.

Data centres

Before the internet, data was mainly stored in the hard drives of our PCs
or on disks. Today information storage is gradually shifting to the "cloud".
The cloud consists of hundreds of warehouse-type buildings called data centres.
These centres are filled with powerful computers called servers. The cloud is
useful because it allows people and businesses to store data on the internet
that would otherwise take up space on their hard drives. But there is a cost.
Data centres use lots of energy in order to operate. They also produce
a great deal of heat and require more energy just to keep them cool.

A waste of power?

Data centres use about 30 billion watts of electricity every year. That's the same as 30 nuclear power plants. A single data centre can use up more power than a medium-sized town. On average only 6 to 12 percent of this energy is actually used by the public at any given time. The rest is used to keep the servers ready for the next surge of activity. Servers must keep everything available, even the parts that are not being used. In other words, keeping every part of the internet instantly available at the click of a mouse is harmful to the environment.

WHAT DO YOU THINK?

How can you limit your use of the internet to help save the planet?

The cost of browsing

Because it's so easy to look something up online, we don't think about the cost. However, even a simple search for "pizza" will suggest websites, Google maps, reviews and recipes. Many machines had to process all this information in a fraction of a second. Doing so requires energy. With more than 100 billion internet searches conducted each month, it all adds up.

Each day internet users perform nearly 6 million Google searches.

Carbon footprint of the internet

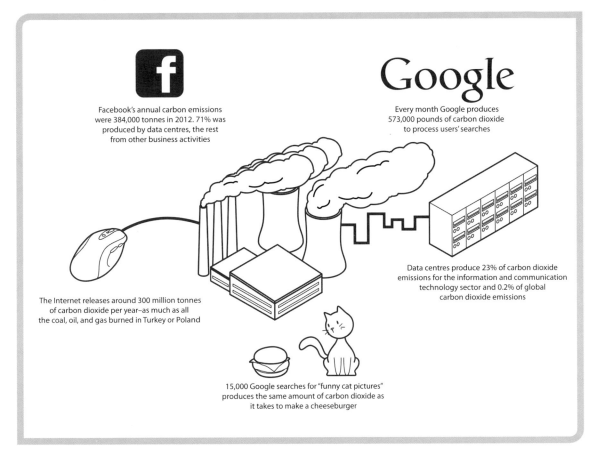

Facebook's annual carbon emissions were 384,000 tonnes in 2012. 71% was produced by data centres, the rest from other business activities

Every month Google produces 573,000 pounds of carbon dioxide to process users' searches

Data centres produce 23% of carbon dioxide emissions for the information and communication technology sector and 0.2% of global carbon dioxide emissions

The Internet releases around 300 million tonnes of carbon dioxide per year–as much as all the coal, oil, and gas burned in Turkey or Poland

15,000 Google searches for "funny cat pictures" produces the same amount of carbon dioxide as it takes to make a cheeseburger

CYBER SENSE

You can reduce your cyber-carbon footprint by:

• using more specific keywords when browsing.

• directly pasting a website address into a browser.

• saving frequently used sites as favourites or bookmarks.

• switching off devices when not using them.

• giving old computers to charities or recycling centres.

The future of the internet and social media

The internet and social media has already had a dramatic impact on society. How might the online world look in the future?

The internet of things

Instead of being a place only accessed through a screen, the internet is likely to become part of all the objects we use. Everything from cars and watches to clothing and medicine may be connected to the internet. Almost any object can be given a web address and then programmed to share data, such as location and temperature. Of course, not everyone may like this new online world. Do we really want our possessions to share the details of our lives on the internet?

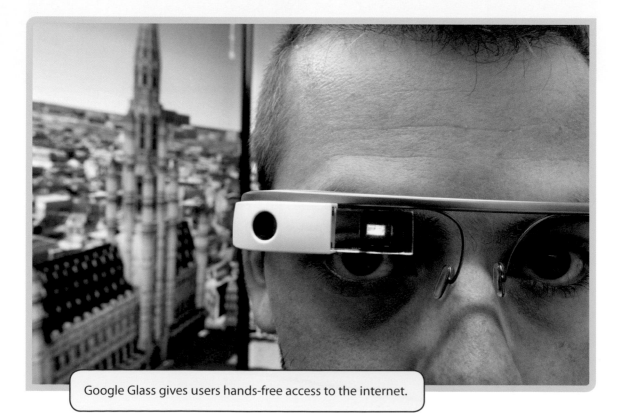

Google Glass gives users hands-free access to the internet.

Schools are now using tablets in the classroom to share information with students.

Online problems

The internet seems to bring out the bad in some people. Lawmakers are changing laws to deal with some of the problems of the internet, such as cyberstalking and online piracy.

Some people believe the internet is already changing how our minds work. Our reliance on the internet for information and entertainment may be reducing our powers of concentration and memory. After all, what's the point of remembering stuff when we can look it up in a search engine? Others argue that the internet is just a tool we can use to get more out of life.

WHAT DO YOU THINK?

What kind of future would you like to see for the internet and social media? What future would you NOT like to see?

Debate it!

Are you ready to debate some of these issues with your friends?
If so, these five tips may help.

1. Be prepared. Do some research before you begin. Make a list of points you plan to debate. Then think of arguments on the other side. Then you'll be prepared when your friend mentions them.

2. State your opinions clearly. It's useful to provide examples and statistics.

3. Listen carefully. After all, you cannot respond effectively unless you understand exactly what your friend is saying. You can ask your friend to repeat the comment or provide further information.

4. Keep your cool. In a good debate there is no clear winner or loser. You will win some points and lose others. You may even find that some of your friend's comments make sense. That's not bad. It shows that you are keeping an open mind.

5. Have fun! Debate is a great way to explore the issues.

Glossary

bias favouring one person or point of view over another

blog online journal that is updated regularly; blog is short for "web log"

brick-and-mortar (shop) physical shop

broadband way of sending large amounts of data over the internet

browser computer program that allows someone to use the internet

cyberbully someone who uses the internet and other forms of electronic communication to bully others

download to copy data from one computer system to another

encrypted changed into a code to prevent unauthorized access

fraud deceiving someone in order to make money

hacker someone who uses computers to gain unauthorized access to data

hard drive part of a computer where data is sorted and stored

hyperlink link from one electronic document or location to another, usually activated by clicking on a highlighted word or image on a screen

hypertext system that links topics on a screen to related information and graphics, usually accessed by pointing and clicking with a mouse

icon symbol on a computer screen that can be clicked on

peer-to-peer file sharing sharing of computer files between computers belonging to private individuals

privacy settings controls on social media sites that allow users to control who is allowed to see what is on their page

scammer someone who tries to trick or deceive people

search engine website that allows users to search for things online

smartphone mobile phone with access to the internet and some computer programs

social network website or application that enables users to communicate with each other by posting information, comments, messages, images and so on

stalker person who gives unwanted or excessive attention to another person

stream to send out data continuously so that it can be viewed or listened to while the remainder is downloading

tablet computer that accepts input directly onto a screen rather than via a keyboard or mouse

upload to transfer data to another computer system

user-generated website site created by members of the public

viral involving rapid spread of information by being circulated on the internet

virtual community internet-based group of people sharing common interests and concerns

Find out more

Books

Internet Crime (Talk About), Sarah Levete (Wayland, 2011)

Internet Safety (Let's Read and Talk About), Anne Rooney
(Sea-to-Sea Publications, 2013)

The Internet and the World Wide Web (Getting the Message), Sean Connolly
(Franklin Watts, 2010)

Websites

www.bbc.co.uk/newsround/13906802
This web page gives information about cyberbullying and how to stop it.

http://www.safetynetkids.org.uk/personal-safety/staying-safe-online/
Learn more about how to stay safe online.

www.thinkuknow.co.uk/11_16/new/social-networking
Find out about social networking and how to use it safely.

Further research

Do some further research on the history of the internet. See if you can find out which was the first:

- website
- browser
- e-shop
- blog
- social network

The next time you research a topic for school or for fun, make a comparison between information gathered on authoritative sites and Wikipedia. Note any differences and make your own evaluation of the accuracy of Wikipedia. If you find mistakes on Wikipedia, help this collaborative project by correcting them. See the Wikipedia introduction site for details.

As internet use expands, some websites are struggling to meet their energy bills. If this continues, it could lead to website failures, communications disruption and possible loss of data. Research what the industry is doing to combat this threat. Typing "green" and "data centre" into a search engine will take you to some interesting articles.

Index